copyright ©2018 by Christopher Broschell.

All rights reserved. No part of this book may be reproduced of transmitted in any form or by any means, electronic or mechanical, including photocopying, recording or by any information storage and retrieval system without permission in writing from the publisher.

ISBN: 978-0-9948396-2-6

First Edition

1.
Antarctica contains about 70 percent of the Earth's fresh water.
Source: American Museum of Natural History.

Sure, it's tied up in ice sheets but there is about 30 million cubic kilometres (or 656,000 cubic miles) of fresh water on top of the continent. Unfortunately, melting it would cause sea levels to go up about 230 feet, which would take out pretty well every coastline in the world.

2.
And 20% of the world's remaining fresh water is in Canada.
Source: Statistics Canada

True, but most of it is tied up in glaciers, ice and underground aquifers. Brazil has three times as much renewable, accessible water as Canada.

3.
The first computer was invented during Thomas Jefferson's lifetime.
Sources: computinghistory.org.uk, brittanica.com

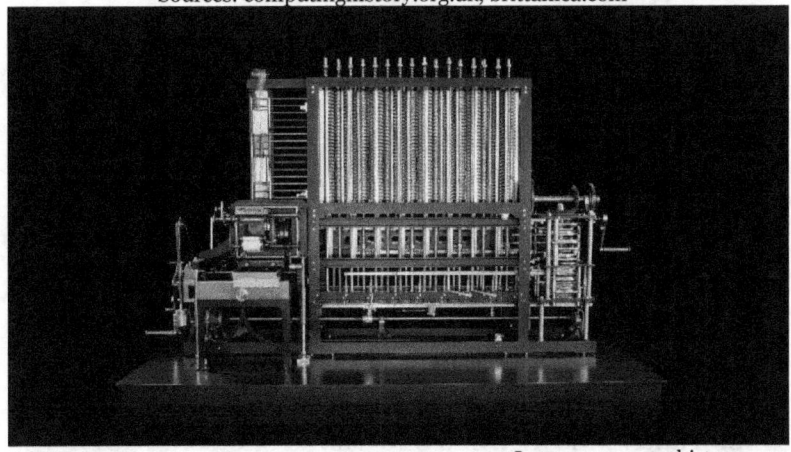

Image: computerhistory.org

In 1823, Charles Babbage started worked on a "automatic computing engine," one year before Jefferson died. Expensive to make, he ran out of money, but in 2002 Babbage's machine was built and is accurate down to 31 decimals.

4.
There is more oil in Venezuela than Saudi Arabia.
Source: worldatlas.com

By country, here are the world's oil reserves:
Venezuela has 300 billion barrels,
Saudi Arabia 266 billion,
Canada 169 billion,
Iran billion,
Iraq billion.

5.
We take more pictures a year as existed in the world up to 1980.
Sources: New York Times, buzzfeed.com

From 1826 to 1980, a low-ball estimate would be 750 billion and at the high end one trillion photos. In 2017, there were an estimated 1.2 trillion photos taken.

6.
The United States has the highest percentage of its population in prison.
Source: prisonstudies.org.

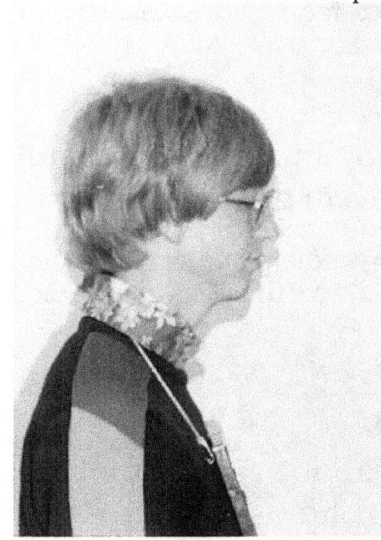

Bill Gates, after a run in with the law.

There are over 2.1 million Americans in prison, about 500,000 more than China, the number 2 country. There are more Americans in jail than the combined population of Philadelphia and Tucson.

7.
It would take 100 hours in wages to buy a TV in 1960. It only took 20 in 2017.
Sources: tvhistory.org and the Bureau of Labor.

A 17" tabletop Philco was $249 and if you had a good manufacturing job, you made $2.57/hr. Fast forward to 2017. A 50" Sony sold for $429 and the average wage was $857 a week.

8.
And in the U.K., you must pay for a TV license.
Source: mirror.co.uk.

It's true, and as of April 1 ,2018, Brits must pay £150.50 a year for a colour license. That money is then sent off to the BBC to pay for the public broadcaster. I guess somebody has to pay for Doctor Who.

9.
More people died in the Spanish flu pandemic following World War I than died in the war.
Sources: *1918 Influenza: the Mother of All Pandemics*, brittanica.com

The cold hard facts: 16 million soldiers and civilians died during the four-year conflict; three times as many died during the one-year epidemic.

10.
The world's oceans hold about 20 million tons of gold. Fort Knox holds 4,582
Source: NOAA

Sure, there is only about one gram of gold for every 100 million metric tons of ocean water in the Atlantic and north Pacific, but there's a lot of water in them thar oceans!

11.
The first vending machine was invented in Egypt around the time of Jesus
Source: Smithsonian Magazine

Invented in the first century by the mathematician Hero, the first vending machine dispensed holy water after you put your coin in. Depending on his travels, Jesus could have stopped by to look.

12.
There were more murders in Chicago in 2016 than all of Canada.
Sources: CNN, Statistics Canada.

In 2016, there were 771 murders in Chicago, but only 611 in all of Canada. By the way, there are 2.7 million people in the Windy City and 36.2 million in the Great White North.

13.
Drug lord Pablo Escobar spent $2,500 a month on rubber bands to bundle his money.
Source: *The Accountant's Story: Inside the Violent World of the Medellín Cartel*

14.
He also lost about $2.1 billion to spoilage
This included being eaten by rats and water damage, but since he was worth over $30 billion, what's a couple of billion here and there.

15.
Heroin was invented by Bayer as a kids' cold medicine.

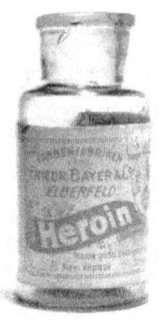

Bayer, inventors of the aspirin, also have a more dubious creation to their credit. In the 1890s, they synthesized heroin for use as a child's cough suppressant.

16.
The largest printer of bibles is in China.
Source: telegraph.co.uk.

Which is kind of funny, since China is officially an atheist country. The Amity Foundation has printed over 125 million copies since 1987.

17.
More Americans own guns than bibles.
Sources: American Bible Society, The Atlantic

There are 87 bibles for every 100 people in the U.S., but there are 88.8 guns for every 100.

18.
More people live in China than the entire western hemisphere

About 1.03 billion people live in the combined North and South America, Iceland, Ireland and those African countries on the west side of the Greenwich Meridian. 1.379 billion live in China.

19.
Beer was invented 2500 years before the wheel.
Source: Smithsonian Magazine.

The earliest beer was created around 3400BC. Compare that to the earliest wheel used to move things, which came around in ancient Greece around 600 BC.

20.
Writing was invented before the alphabet and both were invented before paper
Sources: University of Texas, Encyclopedia Britannica, www.historychannel.com.au

Writing: 3200BC in Mesopotamia,
Alphabet: 1700BC in Phoenicia,
Paper: 105AD in China.
(Vowels, by the way, weren't invented until about 800BC)

21.
Solar power was invented in 1839.
Source: US D.O.E.

Ok, this one is a bit of a stretch, but in 1839, 19-year-old Edmond Becquerel experimented with an electrolytic cell — and realized electricity-generation increased when exposed to light. Sure, it wasn't a solar-powered calculator, but we had to start somewhere.

22.
And plastic was invented in 1869.
Source: sciencehistory.org.

The first synthetic polymer was invented by John Wesley Hyatt, who was inspired by a company's offer of $10,000 for anyone who could provide a substitute for ivory. By treating cellulose with camphor, Hyatt discovered a plastic that could look like ivory.

23.
World War II hasn't ended yet.
Source: Christian Science Monitor.

Russia and Japan still refuse to sign a peace treaty after Russia declared war on Japan in August 1945. Their bone of contention is Japan wants the Kuril Islands back; Russia says no.

24.
Jeff Bezos has enough money to buy every MLB team, Ford and a Hawaiian island
Sources: Google, Forbes

The founder of Amazon has a net worth (as of March 2018) of $130 billion. According to Forbes, the average Major League Baseball team is worth $1.3 billion and with 30 teams, that's only a pitiable $39 billion. That leaves Jeff $91 billion, with which he would have enough money to buy Ford ($42 billion), Delta Airlines ($40 billion) and then purchase a Hawaiian island (Larry Ellison bought Lanai for $300 million, so not too far-fetched).

25.
If every American peed in the shower, we would save 185 billion gallons of water a year.
Source: iflscience.com

Of course, that's not considering those of us who pee in the shower already.

26.
You are more likely to be killed taking a selfie than by a shark
Sources: Forbes, Florida Museum of Natural History

In the first eight months of 2016 there were 73 selfie-related deaths in the world but only five shark-related. As an interesting side note, since 1978, 37 people have been killed by vending machines.

27.
Although you are more likely to be attacked by a shark than catch the plague
Sources: CNN, CDC.

In 2015 there were 59 shark attacks in the United States and 16 cases of the bubonic plague (yep, the same one that wiped out one third of Europe's population in the Middle Ages).

28.

George Washington was the only president to receive all electoral college votes. Twice.

But only 43,782 people voted for him (out of a population of about 3.9 million). By the way, no president has ever had more than 50% of the American public vote for them.

29.
The gun death rate is higher in the U.S. than in Syria, Libya or Iran
Source: npr.org

The firearm murder rate in the U.S. is 3.85 people per 100,000, but only 1.17 in Syria, 0.88 in Libya and 0.80 in Iran. Granted, your odds of dying from a tank blowing up your village in Syria is higher and you really must keep your mouth shut in Iran.

30.
The first Apple computer was released a year before the last guillotine execution in France.

Hamida Djandoubi was executed on September 10, 1977 for the torture-slaying of his girlfriend. Not only was he the last man to have his head lopped off in France, he was the last man executed in the country period.

31.
It has snowed in the Bahamas.
Source: bahamaslocal.com

On January 17, 1977 a cold wave came down into southern Florida and brought cold weather all the way to the Bahamas. For the only time in recorded history, snow fell on the city of Freeport on the island of Grand Bahama.

32.
Thomas Crapper invented the toilet.

FALSE! Crapper was a plumber but did not invent the flush toilet (it had already been around for almost 100 years when he came along). He did invent the bathroom showroom though.

33.
Russia has a larger surface area than Pluto.
Sources: NASA, brittanica.com

Pluto's surface area is 16,647,940km², Russia's is 17,098,200. That's right, Russia's big enough to be its own (dwarf) planet.

34.
Oxford and Cambridge have been around since the Roman Empire.

Technically yes, but we are talking the Eastern Roman Empire, when the boys moved to Constantinople after Rome fell in 476. So yes, the Roman Empire did exist when Oxford was founded (in 1188) and Cambridge (1209).

35.
The unicorn is Scotland's national animal
Sources: National Geographic, USA Today, visitscotland.com

I seriously had to look this one up three times.

36.
Strawberries and raspberries aren't berries. Bananas and eggplants are.

In the botanical sense, of course. True berries are simple fruits stemming from one flower with one ovary and typically have several seeds.

37.
Tomatoes are a fruit, but legally a vegetable in the U.S.

This one goes back to 1893, when the U.S. Supreme Court ruled in favor of a tax collector, who claimed tomatoes were veggies, therefore subject to higher taxes.

38.
Almonds produce cyanide.
Source: brittanica.com

There are two types of almonds: sweet, which are eating almonds and bitter, which are used for almond extract. The bitter almonds must have the hydrogen cyanide removed first – this is why the old murder mysteries used to have the "ah yes, I smelled bitter almonds" when the victim was poisoned.

39.
Ford and GM made most of the military trucks for the Nazis
Sources: Internal Ford documents, Henry Ashby Turner

In Ford's own research, the company recognized their German division had made one third of the heavy military trucks the Nazis used during World War II. General Motors Opel division, made another 45%, leaving less than a quarter for the German companies.

40.
Donald Trump is the only president to never hold elected office.

FALSE! Even if you take out the war heroes (Eisenhower, Grant, Taylor and Washington), Herbert Hoover and William Taft never held elected office.

41.
Teflon was invented accidentally
Source: sciencehistory.org

Roy J. Plunkett froze a mix of chemicals, hoping to find a better refrigerant. He found the chemicals wouldn't leave the cylinders they were in and nothing would stick to them.

42.
And Velcro was invented by a man after walking his dog in the woods
Source: Christian Science Monitor.

George De Mestral and his unnamed dog were taking a walk and George noticed burs sticking to his clothes and the dog. He looked at the burs under a microscope and noticed the tiny hooks which stuck to his fuzzy clothes.

43.
Elisha Gray was possibly the true inventor of the telephone.

In one of those flukes of history, Alexander Graham Bell's lawyer filed a patent for the phone in the morning of February 14, 1876. According to urban legend, Gray's lawyer dropped off the patent application on the same day, but being Valentine's Day, dropped off a love note to his wife first, delaying the application.

44.
An octopus has three hearts.
Source: Smithsonian magazine.

Two of the hearts work exclusively to move blood beyond the animal's gills, while the third keeps circulation flowing for the organs.

45.
A blue whale is as long as a Boeing 737 and weighs 3 times as much
Sources: National Geographic, Boeing.

A blue whale grows up to 100 feet long and weigh 200 tons. A Boeing 737-100 meanwhile was 94 feet long and only weighed 46 tons.

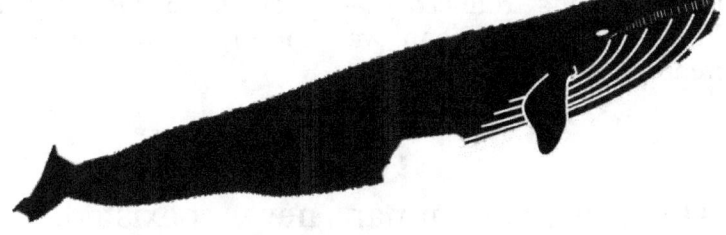

46.
Napoleon wasn't short.

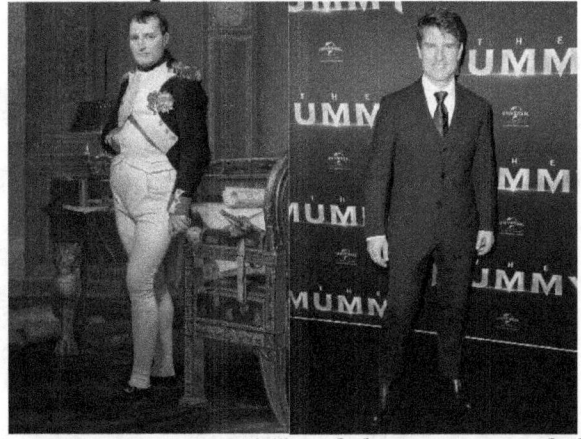

Monsieur Bonaparte was 5'6" and the average male height at the time was 5'5." So really, Nappy was taller than average for his time. But in perspective, he was about the same height as Tom Cruise.

47.
The Great Wall of China is visible from space
Source: NASA, Scientific American.

FALSE! We can pretty well rely on NASA to tell us what you can and can't see from space. The myth comes from a 1932 *Ripley's Believe it or Not* cartoon which said you could not only see the Great Wall in space but even from the moon. Lunar astronauts trounced that theory by saying all you could see from the moon was continents, oceans and splotches of white on blue.

48.
Dinosaurs and humans never coexisted.

Sorry *Flintstones*. Dinosaurs died out 65 million years ago. The first human-like creatures appeared about 6 million years ago and homo sapiens (you and me) only about 200,000 years ago.

49.
Caffeine doesn't dehydrate you.
Source: The Mayo Clinic.

Drinking coffee makes you pee, but it doesn't increase the risk of dehydration.

50.
Mauna Kea is the tallest mountain in the world.
Source: livescience.com.

Ah yes, Mt. Everest is tall. So very, very tall. It is 29,035 feet tall. But Mauna Kea is 33,500 feet tall, you just can't see the 19,700 feet buried in the Pacific Ocean.

51.
The Great Pyramid was the tallest building in the world for 3,800 years

At 481 feet, it held the record from about 2560BC to 1311AD. The Burj Khalifa would have to be the tallest building until the year 5879 to beat this record.

52.
Lemmings don't run off cliffs.
Source: Alaska Dept. of Fish & Game.

An urban legend perpetuated by some nasty people working for Disney. A 1958 short movie called *White Wilderness*, part of the studio's *True Life Adventure* series, featured a segment on lemmings, detailing their strange compulsion to commit mass suicide. The scenes were faked and the lemmings were actually thrown off a cliff by the Disney filmmakers.

53.
Eve didn't give Adam the apple.

Nowhere in the book of Genesis is an apple mentioned. The confusion comes from translation from Latin to English. The Latin word for evil is *mali* and apple is *malum*. The biblical verse is "of the tree of the knowledge of good and evil thou shall not eat." Somebody translated that as "good and apple" and it has stuck ever since.

54.
We use 100% of our brains.
Source: Scientific American.

That old wives' tale about only using 10% of our brain – hogwash! The myth probably comes from Albert Einstein, who used it to explain his towering intellect.

55.
Witches in Salem weren't burned at the stake.
Source: history.com.

Witches in Salem were hanged (19 in all), not burned at the stake. That practice was used in Europe during the Middle Ages.

56.
Mike the headless chicken lived for 18 months without its head
Sources: bbc.com, Smithsonian, Time.

In September 1945, Lloyd Olsen was preparing chickens for sale, cut the head off Mike, but Mike kept on going...for 18 months, dying in an Arizona motel room in 1946 while a member of a circus sideshow.

57.
The Greenland shark can live up to 400 years.
Source: livescience.com

Scientists tested eye tissue from this Arctic predator and found the oldest they tested ranged from 335 to 392 years old, which means they were born around the time the Pilgrims landed at Plymouth Rock.

58.
Turkeys can spontaneously impregnate themselves.
Source: U.S. Dept. of Agriculture.

In 1953, scientists segregated 23 virgin turkey hens for nine months. During that time, the turkeys laid 1,463 eggs without the help of male turkeys.

59.
Nintendo was founded in 1889.

Yep, the video game behemoth was founded September 23, 1889 in Kyoto, Japan as a playing card company. Super Mario didn't come around until almost 100 years later.

60.
There is a tree in India bigger than a Walmart.
Source: atlasobscura.com.

The Great Banyan Tree in Kolkata, India is about the size of a forest, covering 155,000 square feet. The average Walmart covers about 104,000 square feet.

61.
Cleopatra lived closer in time to the Tesla 3 than the building of the Pyramids

Cleo was born in 69BC, 2086 years before the Tesla 3. The Great Pyramid of Giza was started around 2470BC, 2401 years before the birth of the Egyptian queen.

62.
A day on Venus is longer than a year on Venus
Source: space-facts.com.

One rotation of the planet (which we consider a day) takes the equivalent of 243 Earth days, but it circles the sun (which we consider a year) every 225 Earth days.

63.
Viking helmets did not have horns.

Thanks to a Wagner opera in the 1800s and some imaginative costume designers, everyone thinks Vikings attached horns to their helmets. Vikings wore either leather or iron helmets – no horns.

64.
Gum does not take 7 years to digest.
Source: Scientific American.

Nope, the sweeteners are broken down by the body and the gum base just shoots through the digestive tract.

65.
Einstein didn't fail math.
Source: Washington Post.

Yeah, another urban legend to make people feel better. Einstein did fail his entrance exam to Zurich Polytechnic when he was 16, but the exam was in French and his French sucked.

66.
Dinosaurs had feathers.
Source: National Geographic.

Sorry *Jurassic Park*, but it seems almost all dinosaurs had feathers. Fossils show the T-Rex, however, was covered in scales, not feathers.

67.
And they weren't cold-blooded.
Source: Nature.

This is an interesting one. Dinosaurs were neither warm-blooded or cold-blooded but somewhere in between. Not sure what's in between, but I'm not a scientist either (tepid-blooded, perhaps?)

68.
If the lifespan of the Earth were compressed into 24 hours, the first humans appeared at 11:59:56pm.
Source: flowingdata.com.

Seems the Earth was pretty well abandoned until 5:36am, the dinosaurs didn't show up until almost 11 at night and we've only been here for about $1/20000^{th}$ of the Earth's existence.

69.
The highest temperature swing in one day is 100°F (56°C)
Source: Guinness Book of World Records.

In January of 1916 in Browning Montana, the temperature fell from 44°F to -56°F literally overnight.

70.
Spain's national anthem has no words.

FALSE! This one floats around the internet like an old rubber ducky. The Spanish national anthem does have words, but Spaniards ridicule the idea of lyrics and the idea hasn't caught on.

71.
The color orange was named after the fruit.
Sources: Merriam Webster, independent.co.uk.

The color is named after the color of the fruit and interestingly, many languages don't have a word for the magical mix of red and yellow.

72.
French was the official language of England for 300 years.
Source: thehistoryofenglish.com.

When William the Conqueror crossed the English Channel from France in 1066, he brought with him his language. This changed in 1362 when the Statute of Pleading made English the official language of England (though the statute was written in French).

73.
Cats have two sets of vocal cords: one for purring and one for meowing.
Source: petmd.com.

A cat's vocal cords have an additional membrane called the ventricular cords which are used for purring. They can vibrate these rapidly without closing the trachea completely and can breathe when they are purring.

74.
Giraffes have no vocal chords.
Source: USA Today.

FALSE! Scientists originally thought giraffes had no vocal cords, as they could only discern a grunt or a snort. After analysing 97 hours of giraffe recordings, they realized giraffes were communicating at infrasonic levels (in other words, below human hearing).

75.
Penguins have an organ above their eyes which converts seawater to fresh water.
Source: Smithsonian Magazine.

Though they drink in a lot of seawater, penguins have a supraorbital gland which filters the salt, which the penguins remove from their bodies by sneezing.

76.
And speaking of sneezing, one can travel up to 100mph.
Source: livescience.com, American Lung Association.

Although *Mythbusters* claims this is false, I'll take the word of the American Lung Association. Since most particles ejected from your mouth can't be seen by the human eye, it's easy to see where *Mythbusters* got this wrong.

77.
Uhura stayed on *Star Trek* because of one fan.
Source: npr.org.

Nichelle Nichols, who portrayed Uhura on the original series, was ready to pack her bags and head back to Broadway until a fan asked her to stay. The fan was Dr. Martin Luther King and he asked her to stay to be a role model for future generations, because he believed Gene Roddenberry's vision was how humanity was supposed to be.

78.
The word "sinister" means left-handed.
Yes, those southpaws out there were considered evil back in the day. Sinister comes from the Middle English word *sinestre* (on the left) and Latin *sinister manus* (left hand)

79.
Every panda in the world is the property of the Chinese government.
Source: LA Times.

The Chinese government rents out pandas to various zoos around the world for about $575,000 a year. The Smithsonian Zoo had two giant pandas born there in 2015, which when they reach sexual maturity, will return to China to increase the breeding stock of the endangered animal.

80.
An acre of trees produces enough oxygen for 18 people.
Source: Growing Air Foundation

81.
In 1923, a dead jockey won a horse race.
Source: Guinness Book of World Records.

Sound like a *National Enquirer* headline, but it is a true story. Poor ol' Frank Hayes was riding Sweet Kiss at Belmont when he had a heart attack mid-race and died. His body stayed in the saddle until his horse crossed the line for a 20–1 longshot. Imagine the ribbing in the clubhouse after – *you lost to a dead guy!*

82.
The record time between twins being born is 87 days.
Source: mirror.co.uk.

Again, sounds like something from the tabloids, but Maria Jones-Elliott went into labor four months early, delivered one child, then the other stayed in the womb for almost three more months. (The previous record, by the way, was 84 days so maybe not too farfetched).

83.
Kangaroos have three vaginas.
Source: Discover Magazine.

Don't even know what to say about this one. Sperm travels up the two side vaginas and the joeys travel down the middle one. Wow.

84.
The U.S. Mint loses about $40 million a year making pennies.
Sources: CBS News, Smithsonian Magazine.

The Mint makes 9.1 billion pennies a year at an average cost of 1.43 cents for every penny, so you do the math.

85.
There is a family in Kentucky with blue skin.
Source: ABC News.

The Fugate family of Kentucky carry a rare blood disorder known as methemoglobinemia which causes their lips, nails and skin to turn blue. Through inbreeding in the 1800s, a small community of blue-skinned people developed but in recent years (since both parents must carry the recessive gene) it is very rare.

86.
The Great Sphinx was already 900 years old when the last woolly mammoths died out.

There may not have been dinosaurs and humans walking together, but mankind had already built the Great Sphinx in Egypt when they were still hunting the woolly mammoth to extinction. The Sphinx dates to about 2550BC and the last mammoths still lived on Wrangel Island in the Arctic in 1650BC.

87.
O.J. Simpson was supposed to play the Terminator.
Source: Entertainment Weekly.

The studio head wanted The Juice to play the Terminator in the 1984 classic, but director James Cameron didn't think he could be a remorseless killer. "This was when everybody loved him—he was this likable, goofy, kind of innocent guy. Plus, frankly, I wasn't interested in an African-American man chasing around a white girl with a knife."

88.
The world's eight richest men are as rich as the poorest bottom half of the population.
Sources: Oxfam, Forbes.

From bottom to top, they are:
- Charles Koch: $60.3 billion
- David Koch: $60.3 billion
- Larry Ellison: $61.2 billion
- Amancio Ortega: $65.6 billion

- Carlos Slim: $68.7 billion
- Mark Zuckerberg: $71.2 billion
- Warren Buffett: $86.6 billion
- Bill Gates: $90.6 billion
- Jeff Bezos: $130 billion

For a grand total of $694.5 billion, or more than the bottom 3.5 billion of the population. In the United States, Gates, Buffett and Bezos have a larger combined wealth than the bottom 160 million of Americans.

89.
Sure, Jeff Bezos is rich, but he isn't even close to the richest American of all time.
Sources: cnbc.com, time.com

The meter keeps running on the Amazon kingpin, but when you compare his wealth to the Gross Domestic Product of the United States, Bezos is only worth 0.6%. John D. Rockefeller's wealth in 1918 compared to GDP was almost two percent of the country's economic output, or the equivalent of $353 billion. When Andrew Carnegie sold U.S. Steel to J. P Morgan in 1901, the purchase price was equal to 2.1% of GDP, or $390 billion in today's dollars.

90.
Green Eggs and Ham was written as a bet.
Source: snopes.com.

Dr. Seuss' editor Bennett Cerf dared the author to write a book using no more than 50 different words. He did, and the classic was born.

91.
The 1904 Olympic Games included greased pole climbing and mudslinging
Sources: history.com, Smithsonian Magazine

The organizers of the St. Louis games also held *Anthropology Days* where pygmies, American Indians and other natives were kept in a replicated native habitat so Caucasians could stand and gawk at the savages. The "savages" were then recruited to compete in feats such as the greased pole event and mudslinging. Way to go, guys!

92.

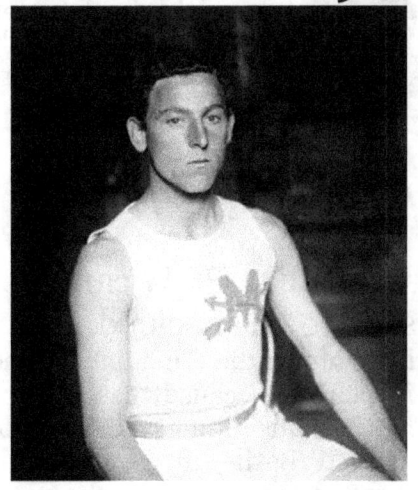

And the guy who won the '04 marathon drove half the race.
Source: Smithsonian Magazine.

Fred Lorz ran some of the St. Louis Olympic marathon but was disqualified when they realized he had ridden in a car for a large chunk of the race.

93.
Coral reefs are the largest living structures on Earth and some are visible from space.
Source: NOAA.

Remember how you can't see the Great Wall from space? Well, you can see the Great Barrier Reef off the coast of Australia, and it's alive.

94.
Coconut water can be used to intravenously hydrate a person.

Source: National Institute of Health.

During World War II when IV saline was in short supply, the legend goes coconut water worked. Since then, there is one case of it working on a man in the Solomon Islands. Not exactly conclusive, but there it is.

95.
Germans held at a Canadian POW camp were politely asked to be shackled.

At Camp 30 in Bowmanville, Ontario the Canadians asked the Germans to be held in chains, because that dastard Hitler did it to our boys. The Germans didn't take kindly to it, and the ridiculously named Battle of Bowmanville ensued. The Germans barricaded themselves in the mess hall and defended themselves with hockey sticks (of course). One Canadian soldier was injured by a flying jar of jam.

96.
A waterfall in Hawaii flows up instead of down.
Source: onlyinhawaii.org.

The Upside-Down Waterfall flows over the edge of a cliff on Mount Konahuanui, then winds catch the falling water and push it up before it reaches the bottom, creating the illusion the falls is flowing in reverse.

97.
The Bloodhound is the only animal whose evidence is admissible in court.

Specifically, in the case of South Carolina v. White, "courts generally admit evidence that bloodhounds tracked down a defendant if the prosecution can establish that the bloodhounds
(1)...are of pure blood, characterized by acuteness of scent and power of discrimination;
(2)... have been trained to pursue human tracks;
(3)...have been found reliable in such pursuit; and
(4)...were put on the trail of the guilty party, which was pursued and followed to give substantial assurance of identification.

98.
It takes about 3,000 cows to supply enough leather for the NFL for only one year.
Source: bleacherreport.com

99.
The bee hummingbird weighs less than a penny.

Which makes it smaller than the largest bee, the elusive Wallace's Giant Bee, which has a wingspan of 2 ½."

100.
The boomslang snake venom kills you by causing you to bleed out of every orifice.
Thankfully, not a common snake, though noted herpetologist Karl Schmidt found out the hard way. In 1957, one day after being bitten by one on the thumb, Schmidt went into respiratory failure and cerebral hemorrhage and died. Interestingly, Marlin Perkins (yes, the guy from *Mutual of Omaha's Wild Kingdom*) sent him one for identification. It didn't go well.

101.
A cat sleeps upwards of 20 hours a day.
Source: Animal Planet.

Cats are predators and in the wild have a lot of chasing to do. This takes lots of energy, which means cats have evolved into lean, mean, sleeping machines, saving up the strength to catch dinner.

102.
Procter & Gamble claims Pringles aren't potato chips.
Let's be clear on this one though – it was a tax dodge. In Britain, chips (or crisps, as the Brits like to call them) are taxed as junk food. In a clearly brilliant move, P&G claimed they weren't chips, so no tax. But if they aren't chips, what are they?

103.
That red dye in your food probably came from ground-up bugs.
Cochineal extract – Red Dye #4 – is made from the ground up insect bodies which are then boiled in ammonia or

sodium carbonate. You will find the bug extract in artificial crab meat, ketchup, soft drinks, yogurt, candy, ice cream, maraschino cherries, lipstick and some pills. Yum!

104.

And artificial vanilla comes from beaver asses.
Source: National Geographic, snopes.com, Huffington Post

Yum again! Beaver butts secrete a goo called castoreum, which the animals use to mark their territory. However, it is quite rare now, since it is prohibitively expensive to collect the stuff and is used mainly in the fragrance industry. **What's used today is much grosser: a distillate of wood-tar creosote.**

105.

Tea bags were invented by accident.

In 1908, New York tea merchant Thomas Sullivan sent samples of tea to his customers in small silken bags. Proving consumers then are as smart as now, some of them just threw the whole bag in their hot water and blimey! the tea bag was invented.

106.

Dogs can smell cancer.
Source: CNN.

Lucy the lab (ha, get it – a lab test!) from Great Britain is one of eight dogs being used in a survey to see if dogs can sniff cancer from urine tests. Lucy, by the way, had a 95% success rate when looking for cancer.

107.

Thomas Jefferson and John Adams both died on the same day.

The two Founding Fathers not only died on the same day, but they died 50 years to the day of the signing of the Declaration of Independence, July 4, 1826 (cue *Twilight Zone* music).

108.

And the last surviving Founding Father died exactly five years later.

James Monroe died on July 4, 1831, 55 years after the Declaration of Independence was signed.

109.

The First Family is expected to pay while at the White House.

Source: CNN.

And you thought it was a free ride. According to former First Lady Laura Bush, a bill came monthly, itemizing everything she and her family owed, including food, dry cleaning and hourly wages for waiters and cleanup crews at private parties.

110.
Aldous Huxley and C.S. Lewis both died the same day as J.F.K.

Huxley, the author of *Brave New World* and Lewis, the man who gave the world the *Chronicles of Narnia*, both died November 22, 1963.

111.
Cellphones have 10 times more germs than toilet seats.
Source: Time.

Ewwww, you people are using them while you're eating. Americans check their phones about 47 times a day, and rarely wash their hands before doing so.

112.
Orange juice is artificially flavored to taste like oranges.
Source: The New Yorker.

Wait, doesn't orange juice taste like orange juice already? Apparently not, and companies add ethyl butyrate to make it taste more...orangy.

113.
Ketchup was originally sold as medicine.
Source: Ripley's.

Now ketchup wasn't ketchup back in the day. It was usually a mix of mushrooms or fish. In 1834 Dr. John Cooke Bennet added tomatoes and claimed it could cure diarrhea, indigestion, jaundice and rheumatism. Sadly, it can't.

114.
A pearl will dissolve in vinegar.
According to legend, Cleopatra drank a mix of pearl and vinegar. The legend is true! Prudence Jones of Montclair State University found you can dissolve a one-gram pearl in supermarket vinegar in about 24 hours.

115.
You can use peanuts to make dynamite.
But you wouldn't. Peanut oil can be processed to produce glycerol, used to make nitroglycerin, a key constituent of dynamite, but it's terribly inefficient.

116.
Clint Eastwood starred in and sang in the western musical *Paint Your Wagon*.
And his marquee song from the movie was "I Talk to the Trees, But They Don't Listen to Me."

117.
The microwave was invented by accident.
Source: Popular Mechanics.

No, there wasn't a bunch of guys standing around, trying to figure out a better way to pop popcorn. Percy Spencer was trying to make a better magnetron using microwaves when he realized his chocolate bar had somehow melted in his pocket. He thought about it, then put an egg underneath the microwave tube. It exploded in his face. The next day he brought in some corn kernels and lo and behold, microwave popcorn was invented as well.

118.
Ice cream is sometimes thickened with seaweed.

Carageenan is derived from red seaweed and though it's not toxic or bad for you, it is thought to contribute to inflammation and stomach irritation.

119.
Star Wars is closer in time to World War II than to the present.

Well isn't that an eye opener. *Star Wars* debuted 32 years after the end of the Second World War and 41 years ago today. If you want a better one, *Star Trek* came out closer to the *First* World War than today.

120.
Ostriches are faster than Usain Bolt.
Source: speedofanimals.com.

Betcha didn't see that one coming. An ostrich hits a top running speed of 70km/h, while Usain Bolt can only go 44.72km/h.

121.
A peregrine falcon can travel faster than a Nascar racer.

Bill Elliott holds the record at Talladega, going 212mph in qualifying. A peregrine falcon, meanwhile, will reach diving speeds of 242mph when it is hunting.

122.
And a horsefly can travel up to 90mph.
Source: speedofanimals.com.

The common horsefly, which has an awful bite to it, has been recorded flying at a dizzying 90 miles per hour.

123.
In Alaska, it is illegal to whisper in someone's ear while they are moose hunting.
Source: onlyinyourstate.com.

But sneaking up behind them and startling them is ok.

124.
Cow farts contribute to climate change.
Source: NASA.

Yes, farts are hilarious, but what isn't funny is that in 2011 alone, cows, sheep, pigs, etc. added 119 million tons of methane into the atmosphere. Big deal, you say? Methane is 25 times worse as a greenhouse gas than carbon dioxide.

125.
A group of crows is a murder.
A group of owls is a parliament.

And A Flock of Seagulls sang *I Ran*.

126.
Monarch butterflies are poisonous to birds.

Monarchs are known to eat poisonous plants when they are caterpillars, which makes them poisonous to birds after they change into butterflies.

127.
A baby kangaroo is the size of a grain of rice when born.
Source: livescience.com.

A kangaroo is pregnant for only about 30 days, gives birth to the joey (which might only be 0.2" long), then keeps him or her in her pouch for another 120 to 450 days.

128.
Five times as many people die from hippo attacks in a year than lion attacks.
Source: telegraph.co.uk.

Yes, those hungry, hungry hippos are just plain ornery. On average, 500 people are killed by hippopotami, but only 100 from lion attacks (which is the same number for elephant attacks, by the way). Freshwater snails are much deadlier, killing about 10,000 people a year.

129.
Washington's teeth were made from slave teeth, not wood.
Source: Washington's papers.

According to George's own ledgers from Mount Vernon, there is a line item for payment: "By Cash pd Negroes for 9 Teeth on Acct of Dr. Lemoire." Dr. Lemoire was Dr. Jean Le Mayeur, Washington's dentist.

130.
There is a caterpillar whose fuzzy hairs will kill you.
Source: http://www.scielo.br/scielo.php?pid=S0365-05962005000700002&script=sci_arttext&tlng=en

The caterpillar of the giant silkworm moth is responsible for several human deaths each year. Its hairs release a potent toxin that is poisonous.

131.
Humans share 99.9% DNA with other humans.
So can't we all just get along?

132.
And 60% with chickens and bananas.
Source: getscience.com.

Many of the "housekeeping" genes that are necessary for basic cellular function, such as for replicating DNA, controlling the cell cycle, and helping cells divide are shared between many plants (including bananas) and animals.

133.
Mosquitoes have killed more humans than all the wars in history combined.

FALSE! According to the World Health Organization, mosquitoes kill about 725,000 every year, so from 1900-2017 that would be 84,825,000 people. World War I killed about 20 million; World War II another 60 million, Vietnam another 2 million, the Korean War another 1 million, Iran-Iraq 600,000, Rwanda 500,000, Afghanistan 500,000, Syria 185,000, Angola 114,000 – we're already over the WHO number and those are just the larger conflicts.

134.
There is a road in Japan which plays music as you drive over it.
Source: theguardian.com.

A team from the Hokkaido Industrial Research Institute has built several "melody roads," which use cars as tuning forks to play music as they travel.

135.
Male sea horses give birth to the young.

So we men DO know the pain of pregnancy – or at least we men sea horses.

136.
A donkey can see all four feet at the same time.
Source: rosamondgiffordzoo.org

Because of the wide spacing of the eyes on its head, a donkey has a nearly 360-degree view of their surroundings, including all four feet.

137.
An elephant's trunk contains over 40,000 muscles.

FALSE! This information dates to the early 1800s and modern scientists believe there are seven major muscles and many "sub-muscles," but not 40,000.

138.
And elephants can smell water up to 12 miles away
Source: Seaworld

139.
Scallops have 100 eyes.
Source: The Optics of Life: A Biologist's Guide to Light in Nature

Since we only eat the muscle of the scallop with our fettucine, most people don't realize the scallop has an amazing number of ocular organs.

140.
Nearly a third of women over 70 are still sexually active.
Source: Science Daily.

And, according to the AARP, 20% of men and 12% of women over 45 still have oral sex once a week.

141.
The United States has the highest divorce rate on the planet.

FALSE! According to both the Guinness Book and telegraph.co.uk, the U.S. comes in at number 4 or 5 (depending on which one), with Russia, Belarus, Aruba and the Maldives having higher rates.

142.
Palm trees grow in Switzerland.

Around Lake Lugano in the south of Switzerland, you can travel along palm tree-lined boulevards in the land of chocolate.

143.
A starfish spits out its stomach to eat.
Source: Queen Mary University of London.

A starfish will extend its stomach out of its mouth and over the digestible parts of its prey, then partially digests it outside the body before bringing it back in.

144.
Pennsylvania is misspelled on the Liberty Bell.
Source: National Science Foundation.

Oopsie, seems the boys spelled it with one "n," although the NSF claims it "was one of several acceptable spellings of the name at that time." Sure it was.

145.
Red does not make bulls angry.
Source: livescience.com.

Everyone knows the scene – the matador with the red cape making the bull charge. It is not, however, the color which gets the bull going – it's the movement of the cape.

146.
About two dozen people are killed each year by champagne corks
Sources: glassofbubbly.com.

147.
Pope Pius XII died after a bout of uncontrollable hiccups.

This is an interesting one. Pius suffered from long bouts of hiccups, but the actual cause of death was a stroke. Did the hiccups bring on the stroke? Doubtful.

148.
The highest and lowest points in the continental U.S are only 76 miles apart.
This would be much less interesting if the country was flat. Both in California, the highest point is Mount Whitney at 14,505 feet above sea level and the lowest is the Badwater Basin in Death Valley at 279 feet below sea level.

149.
Humans evolved from apes.
FALSE! Humans and apes evolved from a common ancestor millions of years ago, but these are two branches of the family tree and humans and apes evolved independently from one another.

150.
The CIA has been researching how to kill people with their cars.
Source: independent.co.uk.

According to the documents released by WikiLeaks, in October 2014 the CIA was researching ways to hack into vehicles to assassinate people without being detected.

151.
Walmart makes a net profit of $1,557,000 per hour.
Source: Nasdaq.

From Walmart's latest income statement – and remember, that's profit, not just they money coming in.

152.
Lightning never strikes the same place twice.
FALSE! Ever been to the Empire State Building?

153.
By the age of 60, most people will have lost about half their taste buds.
Sources: New York Times, NPR.

As with the other senses – sight, smell, hearing – our sense of taste fades with age. The average human has 9,000 taste buds which regenerate on a two-week cycle. Those cells don't regenerate as well after 50 for women and 60 for men.

154.
Pirates of the Caribbean: On Stranger Tides was the most expensive movie of all time.
The 2011 Johnny Depp move cost $397 million, though it did make over $1 billion, so a sound investment for Disney.

155.
There is an oil field in Iraq which has been burning for 2,500 years.
Near Kirkuk in northern Iraq there is a place called the Eternal Fire of Baba Gurgur. It was discovered by Westerners in 1927 and has been burning ever since. Herodotus mentioned Baba Gurgur in his writings 2,500 years ago and some believe the eternal fire is the one described in the Book of Daniel in the Old Testament.

156.
Richard Belzer has played Detective John Munch on ten different TV shows.

And they are:
Law & Order: SVU;
The Unbreakable Kimmy Schmidt;
30 Rock;
The X-Files;
The Wire;
Arrested Development;
Law & Order: Trial By Jury;
The Beat;
Law & Order and
Homicide: Life on the Street – and holds the record for portraying same character for 22 years.

157.
The man who performed the first television recital also was the first to stream a performance over the Internet.

Earl Wild (1915-2010) performed the first live piano recital on TV in 1939 and followed that up almost 60 years later by streaming a live performance in 1997.

158.
Women, pilot whales and killer whales are the only three mammals known to undergo menopause.

Sources: sciencemag.com, The Atlantic

159.

Scotty on *Star Trek* was shot six times during the D-Day invasion.
Source: startrek.com.

James Doohan was a captain in the Royal Canadian Artillery Regiment when he stormed ashore at Juno Beach. Doohan was shot four times in the leg, had his middle finger blown off by another bullet and was shot in the chest by a sixth, though that bullet was stopped by his silver cigarette case.

160.

And Teddy Roosevelt gave a speech after being shot in the chest.
Sources: history.com, Smithsonian Magazine.

Now let's see today's politicians do that! TR was campaigning in 1912 when an unemployed saloon keeper shot him with a .38. The bullet hit his 50-page speech and passed on through, though the double-folded paper slowed the bullet down. He went to the hall and started: "I don't know whether you fully understand that I have just been shot—but it takes more than that to kill a Bull Moose." Teddy finished the speech...with the bullet still lodged in his chest!

161.
Bob Hope's last words were "Surprise me."
The legendary comedian was responding to his wife Dolores' question where he would like to be buried. She picked the San Fernando Mission Cemetery, Los Angeles.

162.
The first U.S. Constitution allowed for Canada to join, no questions asked.
Part XI: Canada acceding to this confederation, and joining in the measures of the United States, shall be admitted into, and entitled to, all the advantages of this union; but no other colony shall be admitted into the same, unless such admission be agreed to by nine states.

163.
Almost three times as many people are buried under Paris than live in Paris.
The catacombs under Paris are home to the bodies of about six million people. Only 2.24 million live aboveground.

164.
One of the extras on *The Exorcist* was also a serial killer.
Paul Bateson, who played a radiologist's assistant in *The Exorcist*, was a convicted murderer who killed and dismembered up to seven gay men in the late '70s.

165.
The movie *Titanic* cost more to film than the actual ship cost to build.

With inflation, the Titanic cost about $174 million. The movie cost $200 million.

166.
Worcestershire sauce is made from dissolved fish.

Oh, Lea & Perrins! Their sauce is made with liquified anchovies. The anchovies – bones and all – are soaked until they are totally dissolved.

167.
Different parts of your tongue detect different tastes.
Source: National Institute of Health

FALSE! All taste sensations come from all regions of the tongue, although different parts are more sensitive to certain tastes.

168.
The dog who played Toto in *The Wizard of Oz* was paid more than the Munchkins.
Source: cbr.com

While disproving the urban legend Judy Garland was paid less than Terry, a cairn terrier, it did prove the other point. The dog was paid $125 a week while the Munchkins were only paid $100. Talk about inequality!

169.
More people live in New York City than in 39 of the 50 states.

New York City has 8.53 million people (according to the U.S. Census) and the #12 state is Virginia at 8.525 million. The populations decrease from there, down to Wyoming at 573,000.

170.
Hitler's deputy Rudolf Hess was the last prisoner held in the Tower of London.

FALSE, but only barely. The Tower had been converted from a prison to a museum and home to the British Crown Jewels by World War II but served as a very public prison for Hess in May of 1941. Hess was only there for a few days, though. The final prisoner was also a Nazi – Josef Jakobs was a spy captured in 1941 and was the last man to be held there, until he was executed at the Tower in August of 1941.

171.

Steven Spielberg submitted *Schindler's List* for his student film requirement to get his B.A.

Source: L.A. Times.

In 2002, Spielberg finished his last course (Natural Science 492) at Cal State Long Beach, then submitted the Oscar-winning movie to fulfil the last requirement of film school. He also had *Jaws* and *Close Encounters of the Third Kind* critiqued to see if he had a "firm grasp of lighting, sound, editing and script management."

172.

Hollywood was originally a drug free town where you couldn't even ride a bicycle on the sidewalks.

Source: Smithsonian Magazine.

When Horace and Daeida Wilcox founded Hollywood in 1887, they hoped it would become a religious community. They banned liquor and offered free land to anyone willing to build a church. Also banned were firearms, speeding, pool halls and bowling alleys as well as riding bikes on the sidewalks.

173.

The shortest war on record lasted an exhausting 38 minutes.

Source: brittanica.com

On August 27, 1896 the British and the sultan of Zanzibar had a disagreement. The British sent a fleet of warships, the Zanzibari countered with a yacht which sank after engaging the cruiser St. George. After the British bombarded the wooden palace, the sultan surrendered – and everyone was home for lunch.

174.
The shortest performance to win an Oscar was under six minutes.

Beatrice Straight won Best Supporting Actress in 1976 for the film *Network*. Anthony Quinn had to drag on for eight minutes as Paul Gauguin in *Lust for Life* (1956) to win his.

175.
Penguins are prostitutes.
Source: BBC.

Researchers have repeatedly observed female penguins exchanging sexual favors with male penguins that aren't their mates in exchange for pebbles they will use to build nests for their babies.

176.
A hospital in London owns the rights to *Peter Pan*.
Source: gosh.org.

The author of the great book, J. M. Barrie, gifted the rights to *Peter Pan* to Great Ormond Street Hospital for Children. In 1998, the British House of Lords granted those rights to the hospital forever, overriding the copyright act.

177.
You can't see a polar bear with night vision goggles.
Source: insidescience.org.

A polar bear's fur insulates them so well, their body heat stays in and infrared (or night vision) doesn't work on them.

178.
The largest cell in the human body is the female egg and the smallest is the male sperm.

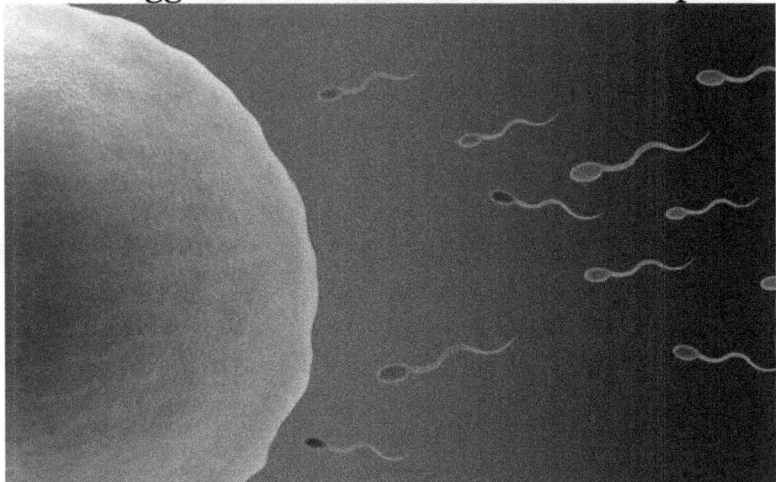

Kind of funny when you think about it.

179.
During your lifetime, you will produce enough saliva to fill two swimming pools.
Sources: webmd.com, livescience.com.

FALSE! The human body produces between two and four pints of spit a day. That equates to about 180 gallons of spit a year and if you live 80 years, 14,400 gallons. An Olympic-sized swimming pool holds 660,000 gallons of water so unless it's two blow-up pools, this is a falsehood.

180.
Jim Caviezel was struck by lightning while filming *The Passion of the Christ*.
Source: BBC.

God is angry, Mel. Very, very angry.

181.
South China Mall is the largest in the world.
Source: forbes.com.

It has 7.1 million square feet of leasable space. By comparison, the largest mall in North America is the West Edmonton Mall, which only has 3.8 million square feet and The Mall of America has a paltry 2.5 million square feet.

182.
The South China Mall is also the largest abandoned mall in the world.

Since opening in 2005, it has averaged a 99% vacancy rate, or about 27 stores for a mall built for 2753.

183.
Babies have 94 more bones than adults.
Source: scienceabc.com.

Babies are born with 300 bones, but by adulthood the number is reduced to 206. Some of the bones get fused into each other, while others are hardened from cartilage, since it would be next to impossible for a woman to deliver a baby whose bones had completely formed.

184.
People in the Middle Ages thought the Earth was flat.
Sources: Newsweek, Washington Post

FALSE! The old crock about Columbus proving the world is round is pure BS. Columbus was looking for the passage to India (hence Caribbean countries called the West Indies) but he wasn't afraid of falling off the Earth. The Earth was believed round as far back as the 6th century BC.

185.

The largest diamond ever discovered weighed 3,106 carats.

That's 1.33 pounds to you and me and would be one hell of an engagement ring. Frederick Wells discovered the largest diamond in South Africa in 1905.

186.

The chimp who played Cheetah in the 1930s *Tarzan* movies outlived both Tarzan and Jane.

Ok, you might be saying big deal, but consider this: the first *Tarzan* movie came out in 1932 and Cheetah was maybe a year old. Johnny Weissmuller died in 1984 and Maureen O'Sullivan died in 1998. Cheetah died in 2011 at the ripe old age of 80 (to compare, the average age of a chimp in the wild is 30 years and in a zoo is 40).

187.

The Roman Empire was not the largest empire in history.

The Roman Empire was only the 24th largest in the world at its height. The British was the largest ever, followed by the Mongol.

188.

The British Empire contained 25% of the world's population and area.

At its height in the 18th century, Great Britain controlled India, Australia, Canada, the future United States and a good chunk of Africa and the Caribbean (which also explains the prevalence of English throughout the world).

189.
Windsor Castle has housed the British royal family since 1070.
Source: Windsor Castle

This makes Windsor the oldest continually occupied home in the world, barely beating out Kirkjubøargarður, which is the oldest wooden house in the world. Built in 1100, it is still home to the Patursson family, or at least the 17th generation of the family, which has lived there since the 1550s.

190.
Every day, the British drink 165 million cups of tea.
Source: The U.K. Tea & Infusions Association.

Which, based on the British population of just over 66 million is about 2 ½ cups of tea a day per person. Since 98% of tea drinkers take it with milk, that's about 630,000 gallons of milk a day, just in their tea.

191.
Pierce Brosnan was forbidden from wearing a tuxedo in any non-James Bond movie.
Source: cinemablend.com.

While Pierce was playing 007 from 1995-2002, he was bound by contract to not wear a tuxedo in any other film.

192.
Over 70% of Americans are overweight.
Source: CDC.

Thankfully obesity only seems to come into play after you turn 20. Under 20, between 17-20% of Americans are overweight. Compare that to Canada, where 54% are overweight, Great Britain (61.7%), Germany (67%) and Japan (23.8%)

193.
Alaska has a longer coastline than all the other states put together.
According to the *Congressional Research Service*, Alaska's coastline is 6,640 miles and the entire U.S. coastline is 12,479 miles, so Alaska contains 53% of the entire country's coastline.

194.

Though grizzly bears are the official animal of California, no grizzly bears have been seen in the wild since 1922.
Kind of like having the unicorn as your national animal, Scotland.

195.
25 million American adults are living with their parents.
According to Pew Research, 32% of the 75.5 million Americans between 18-34 years old are still living in their parents' basement.

196.
A sperm whale's call is louder than a jet talking off.
Source: whales.org.

A sperm whale's call gets up to 230 decibels, while a jet taking off hits 150db. Even when you take the water deadening the sound into consideration, it's still 168db.

197.
Feet have 250,000 sweat glands.
Source: podiatrists.org.

There are 250,000 sweat glands in a pair of feet and they can produce up to half a pint of sweat a day. Yuck.

198.
The killer in *Halloween* wears a William Shatner mask.
Source: startrek.com.

The urban legend is true! The only mask they could find for the movie was a Captain Kirk death mask, which they painted white.

199.
Sex toys are illegal in Alabama.

Under the *Anti-Obscenity Enforcement Act*, it is against the law to "distribute any device designed or marketed for the stimulation of human genital organs." Yes, a dildo could cost you a $10,000 fine or up to a year of hard labor.

200.
It would take 400 years to spend a night in every Las Vegas hotel room.
Source: statista.com.

There are 148,690 hotel rooms in the city itself as of 2017, so yes, it would actually take 407 years to stay in every single one. Again, for a little perspective, it would take you almost 14 years to spend a night in every room – just in the MGM Grand!

201.

There is enough water in Lake Superior
to cover all North and South America
with one foot of water.

Source: Lake Superior Magazine.

To put the Great Lake in perspective, it holds 10% of the world's – yes, the entire world's – surface freshwater. See the picture below – it's that big. There is more water in it than the other four Great Lakes combined.

202.

There's a Darth Vader "gargoyle" on the
National Cathedral in Washington D.C.

Source: Washington National Cathedral.

During a design competition in the 1980s, Christopher Rader submitted a drawing of Lord Vader. The Cathedral accepted, Patrick Plunkett carved it and it sits high atop the northwest tower.

203.

Denver International Airport
is twice the size of Manhattan.
Source: Denver International Airport.

The airport is 53 square miles, Manhattan is only 22, which means Denver is a really, really big airport.

204.

Bourbon barrels in Kentucky outnumber people by more than two million.
Source: Kentucky Distillers' Association.

In 2017, there were 6.6 million barrels of bourbon in the state and only 4.4 million very lucky people.

205.

South Florida is the only place in the world where alligators and crocodiles coexist in the wild.
Source: National Park Service

206.

Every two seconds, a Boeing 737 takes off somewhere in the world.
Source: Boeing

207.

The shortest time as U.S. President is 32 days.
Sources: history.com, brittanica.com

The story goes poor William Henry Harrison gave the longest inaugural address in history in 1841 but neglected to wear an overcoat – which considering the cold March rain that day wasn't smart. Just over a month later, he was dead from pneumonia.

208.
The worst aircraft accident killed 583 people.
In 1977, two fully loaded Boeing 747s carrying over 600 passengers collided in the middle of the runway in the Canary Islands. A KLM 747 tried to take off without clearance, plowing into a PanAm 747 which was taxiing down the runway. Everyone on the KLM flight died, though 61 passengers on the PanAm jet survived having a jumbo jet carve through it.

209.
But on an optimistic note, your odds of surviving a plane crash are 95.7%.
Source: ABC News.

It gets better, nervous flyer. On average, travelers would need to take one flight a day for about 10,000 years before being involved in a fatal crash. So sit, back, relax and have some of those overpriced drinks.

210.
College education in Germany is free for everyone, even if you're not German.
Source: Washington Post.

This was true until recently, when some states started charging non-EU citizens the outlandish sum of $3,500 to study.

211.
The CIA helped put Nelson Mandela in jail.
In 1962, when he was pegged as "the most dangerous Communist outside the Soviet Union," CIA agent Donald Rickard tipped off South African intelligence agents. Mandela was arrested and spent the next 27 years in prison

before becoming the president of South Africa and winning the Nobel Peace Prize.

212.
You have the best odds of living to 100 if you live in Japan.
Source: Newsweek.

Japan has the greatest proportion of its population over 100, with over 60,000 people hitting that mark (that's more than the population of Kissimmee).

213.
If you are 100 now, the odds of you and your spouse still being alive is 1 in 50,000.

But, if you were born in 1970, your odds go up to 1 in 100.

214.
Hawaiians live longer than Mississippians.

Actually, if you live in Hawaii, you have the longest life expectancy (81.2 years) of any state and if you live in Mississippi, it's the shortest at 74.8 years. Must be all the pineapples.

215.
There is a species of crayfish can clone itself.
Source: The Atlantic and others.

Much like those turkeys which can self-impregnate, but the marbled crayfish reproduce like rabbits.

216.
Every *Seinfeld* episode has some reference *to Superman*.
Sources: entertainment.howstuffworks.com, supermanhomepage.com

FALSE! Yes, there is Jerry's Superman doll on the shelf, or magnet on the fridge, but there isn't a reference or mention of Superman, Lois Lane, Lex Luthor or John Williams *Superman* theme in every episode.

217.
Beretta has been making guns since 1526.
Source: beretta.com

That's a long time to be packing heat.

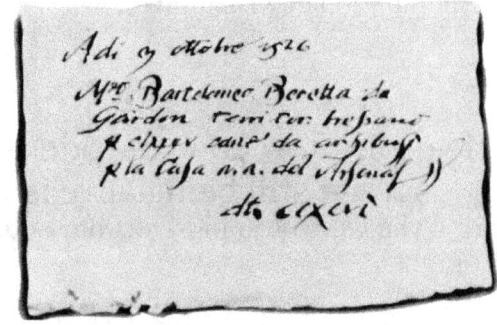

1526 bill of sale for 185 arquebus (precursor to the rifle)

218.
You think that's good, there's a hotel which has been in operation for 1,300 years.
Source: keiunkan.co.jp

The Nisiyama Onsen Keiunkan in Yamanashi, Japan is the oldest continually running business in the world, in operation since 705.

219.
There were 26 assassination attempts on Adolf Hitler.
Source: The Encyclopedia of the Third Reich.

Sadly, none of them successful.

220.
But there were 638 on Fidel Castro.
Now that's according to Cuban officials, but the CIA did have some wacky ideas about how to get rid of him, including the exploding seashell and the poisoned cigar.

221.

Hawaii has a British flag on its flag.
King Kamehameha I had the British flag put on to honor Hawaii's friendship with the British.

222.
Up to 15% of Americans are afraid of seeing the dentist.
Source: Colgate.
That's almost 50 million people

223.
Which might be why dentists are 1.67 times more likely to commit suicide.
Source: Mental Health Daily

If that many people don't like and/or are afraid of you, I'm sure it wears you down.

224.
Only two people jumped out the window during the 1929 Wall Street crash.
Source: Washington Post.

Contrary to Will Rogers, who wrote at the time "you had to stand in line to get a window to jump out of," this urban legend has persisted for almost 90 years.

225.
J. P. Morgan bailed out the U.S. Government in 1895.
Source. J.P.Morgan Chase and others.

Following a Panic in 1893, President Cleveland went to the financier for help. Morgan arranged a bond offering in 1895 to be backed with gold, thus saving the country from financial ruin.

226.
About the same number of Americans believe in God who believe in a J.F.K. conspiracy
Sources: Pew Research, Gallup.

In 2017, 83% of Americans were absolutely or "fairly certain" of the existence of God. The same year, 81% believe Oswald didn't act alone and was part of a broader conspiracy.

227.
Olympic gold medals aren't solid gold.
Source: Time.

Sure you can bite them, but sadly Olympic gold medals are only gold-plated and haven't been solid since 1912. Underneath, they are sterling silver, which you can still bite.

228.
Apple has three times as much cash as the U.S. government
Source: Forbes

It is a fact, but let's put this in perspective: in 2014, Apple had $158 billion in cash on hand, the Treasury had $48.5 billion. The Treasury doesn't keep pallets of hundred-dollar bills lying around, waiting for somebody to need them, and Apple doesn't have a big safe in Steve Jobs old house with $158 billion in it.

229.
A wrong turn killed 80 million people.

Poor Leopold Lojka. In 1914, Leo was driving the Austrian Archduke Franz Ferdinand and his wife down a street in

Sarajevo when he took a wrong turn. When he discovered his mistake, he tried to back up.

The Archduke had just survived an assassination attempt and one of the assassins – Gavrilo Princip – was at a café drowning his sorrows. The car stopped right outside the café. Princip took his semi-automatic pistol and shot both the Archduke and Archduchess. This started World War I and killed 20 million people. The peace terms of World War I were so terrible to the Germans, it enraged Adolf Hitler, who took power, then started WWII and 60 million more dead. See how one wrong turn can change history?

230.
Redheads are going extinct.
Source: howstuffworks.com.

FALSE! Seems this is one of those urban legends perpetuated by big business. Newspapers were reporting on a study done by the official sounding Oxford Hair Foundation that by 2060, the ginger gene was going to disappear, so no more redheads. Seems the Oxford Hair Foundation is funded by Procter & Gamble, makers of Clairol red hair dye.

231.
Bees are covered in hair.
Source: bumblebee.org

Which is how they collect pollen. The pollen sticks to the tiny hairs on a bee's body.

232.
Right-handed people live, on average, nine years longer than left-handed people.

FALSE! Oh my God, don't tell my wife that! The reason given for this is very basic – most machines were devised for right-handed people, so lefties tend to get killed faster. However, the studies from the 1980s proving this have been thoroughly debunked for their research.

233.
The Swiss have bunkers for the entire population in case of a nuclear war.
Source: swissinfo.ch.

Swiss law states everyone must have a protected place they can reach quickly, so many buildings built after 1960 come with fallout shelters.

234.
Donald Trump has belonged to all three political parties.
Source: New York Daily News

In 1987, Trump was a Republican. In 2000, he switched to the Independence Party. In 2001, he switched again to Democrat and in 2009, he switched again to Republican.

235.
Cashews are not nuts and are related to poison sumac.

Cashews are actually seeds and can produce a reaction similar to poison ivy and sumac. This is why you never see raw cashews.

236.
Romania is the most Christian country in the world.
Source: christianityinview.com.

Romania's population is 99.5% Christian and 68 other countries are well above 90%. Christians make up only 78.3% of Americans.

237.
Air pollution from China reaches the U.S.
Source: Smithsonian Magazine.

The irony of this is, a lot of it comes from companies making goods for American consumers.

238.
The longest traffic jam is history was 62 miles and lasted 12 days.
Source: Forbes.

In Beijing, China, people were attempting to take the Beijing-Tibet expressway when the road became clogged with volume of traffic. Again, some brutal irony – a lot of the volume was caused by heavy trucks carrying construction supplies into Beijing for road work intended to help ease congestion.

239.
The acid in your stomach is strong enough to dissolve razorblades.
Source: National Institute of Health.

So who would test this? Thankfully, it was done outside the stomach, but researchers took razorblades, batteries and pennies and left them to soak in stomach acid. (Since people swallow these items, they must research it). The blades were two-thirds dissolved within 24 hours, though the pennies were unaffected (so if you swallow one, it's going to hurt coming out).

240.
Germany has legal say on what babies can be named.
Source: Library of Congress.

FALSE! There are no legal provisions in German law, except parents are only limited if it adversely affects the welfare of the child. The state has a right and a duty to protect the child from an irresponsible name choice. Hence the couple who had to rename their son Lucifer.

241.
But if you live in Iceland, you can only pick certain names.
Source: dw.com.

Icelanders can choose from a list of roughly 1,850 female and 1,700 male names and if that isn't enough, you can appeal to the Icelandic Naming Committee. By the way, they banned the name "Harriet" in 2014.

242.
60% of aircraft tray tables tested positive for an antibiotic-resistant superbug.
Source: CNN.

From one 2007 study of tray tables comes this statistic, so bring an antibacterial wipe before setting your food on a tray someone could've changed a diaper on.

243.
J.F.K. once called himself a donut.

During his famous "Ich bin ein Berliner" speech, but it unfortunately doesn't translate the way Jack was hoping (I am a citizen of Berlin) since a Berliner is a type of donut.

244.
Julia Child was a spy in World War II.
Source: The CIA.

The great French chef Julia Child cooked in a different way in the Second World War. Julia worked for the OSS (The CIA's predecessor) as a research assistant in Washington then later as Chief of the OSS Registry – with top secret clearance to boot. Speaking of cooking, while working there she created a shark repellent which the Navy still uses today.

245.
FedEx has a bigger aircraft fleet than most airlines.

FedEx has the fifth largest fleet of planes in the world (at 634), larger than British Airways, Air France, Lufthansa and Air Canada.

246.
After the Battle of Shiloh in 1862, soldiers' wounds glowed in the dark.
Source: Smithsonian Magazine.

And oddly, those whose wounds glowed seemed to heal better than the others. The mystery was solved in 2001, when it was realized the wounded became hypothermic, and their lowered body temperatures made ideal conditions for a bioluminescent bacterium called *Photorhabdus luminescens*, which inhibits pathogens.

247.
The average life of a paper money is less than five years.
Source: The Atlantic.

All that folding and crumpling takes its toll. The longest-lived bill is usually a $50, which on average lasts 12½ years and the shortest are the $5 and $10, which only stick around under 3½ years.

248.
A farm in Delaware mulches more than four tons of worn-out U.S. cash every day.
Source: Various.

This is a great fun fact, but here's the problem – I can't find any independent verification of this (nobody lists their source) and why would a farm in Delaware need four tons of compost a day?

249.
Arlington National Cemetery used to be Robert E. Lee's estate
Source: arlingtoncemetery.mil.

Lee's wife inherited the estate from her father, who was – ironically – George Washington's step-grandson. At the start of the Civil War, Lee and his wife fled, and in 1863 it was confiscated by the Union for non-payment of $92 in property taxes. The government purchased the land at auction and started turning it into a cemetery. In 1882, their son sued the government (and won), then sold it back to them, since who wants an estate with 6,000 graves on it.

250.
More men died in the Civil War than any other American conflict.
Source: civilwar.org.

About 620,000 men died in the Civil War, more than the TOTAL casualties of both World Wars and Korea.

251.
In World War II, British soldiers got a ration of three sheets of toilet paper a day. Americans got 22.5.
Source: *The American People in World War II: Freedom from Fear, Part Two.*

I just don't know what to say about that.

252.
Penicillin was invented by accident.

Most people know penicillin is mold, but it was discovered when Dr. Alexander Fleming returned from vacation to find his Staphylococcus bacteria was stopped dead in its tracks by some penicillium mold which had made its way to his Petri dishes. That was in 1928, but it wasn't until 1941 it was able to be mass produced.

253.
Corn Flakes were meant to stop masturbation.
Source: forbes.com.

According to John Kellogg, "Highly seasoned meats, stimulating sauces and dainty tidbits irritate the nerves and react upon the sexual organs." So instead of fun foods like steak and potatoes for breakfast, let's try bland corn flakes and stop those juices running.

254.
Your parmesan probably contains sawdust.
Source: bloomberg.com, the FDA.

Mmm, pardon? Cellulose is used in on-the-shelf grated parmesan as an anti-clumping agent (sounds like kitty litter). During an FDA investigation, Castle Cheese, which supplies many chains including Target, actually had ZERO parmesan in its grated parmesan. Walmart's Great Value line had almost 8% cellulose and Kraft had 3.8%.

255.
Oh, and your McDonald's Hot Apple Pie contains duck feathers.
Sources: The Financial Post, theguardian.com.

L-Cysteine is used to soften mass-produced breads and is made from human hair or duck feathers. McDonald's uses the duck feather variety in its Baked Hot Apple Pie and Warm Cinnamon Roll, but most other places use the human hair variety, which is collected from barber shops in China.

256.
Donald Trump has never filed for personal bankruptcy but has filed six Chapter 11 bankruptcies.
Source: snopes.com

So is this a bad thing or a good thing? The Donald has taken down some people with him over the years, going banko on the Trump Taj Mahal, Trump Plaza Casinos, Trump Plaza

Hotel, Trump's Castle, Trump Hotels and Casinos Resorts and Trump Entertainment Resorts.

Now, compare that to companies like Chrysler, Delta, GM and others going into Chapter 11, only to emerge stronger. And, companies like PanAm, Woolworth's and Compaq, which did not.

257.
More Russians died in one World War II battle than the combined American and Britain loss in the entire war.
Source: britannica.com.

The Russians lost a staggering 1.1 million soldiers during the eight-month long siege of Stalingrad by the Nazis in World War II. The United States lost almost 417,000 men and women and the U.K. over 450,000 over the course of the entire war.

258.
Hitler's nephew served in the U.S. Navy during World War II.
Source: americaninwwii.com.

Willy Hitler was in the U.S. on a lecture tour when the war broke out. He tried to enlist, but – I know, hard to believe – he would get turned down because of his last name. He wrote a letter to F.D.R., which was forwarded to J. Edgar Hoover and he was cleared to enlist. In a smart move, he changed his last name after the war to Stuart-Houston, because who wants to be a Hitler?

259.
A Walt Disney film was the first to use the word "vagina."
Sources: YouTube, snopes.com

In 1946, the company produced *"The Story of Menstruation"* to help girls deal with their period (watch it on YouTube). It's also safe to bet it was the first time the word "rectum" was also used on film.

260.
Every two minutes, a woman dies from complications of pregnancy or childbirth.
Source: United Nations Population Fund.

Sadly, this is a vast improvement in the last 30 years. Since 1990, the figure has dropped 44%, but the U.N. calculates 830 women die every day around the world because of this.

261.
Cherries can help you sleep.
Source: nutritionfacts.org.

Specifically, tart cherries, as well as orange bell peppers and walnuts all contain natural melatonin, which can help regulate your sleep cycle as well as help you sleep better. *(Thanks to my 10-year-old daughter for this fun fact!)*

262.
There is a cloud of alcohol in space 1,000 times bigger than our solar system.
Source: sciencealert.com.

In the constellation Aquila, there is a cloud of ethyl alcohol with enough booze in it to supply 300,000 pints of beer every day to every single person on Earth for the next billion years.

263.
At the fastest speed we've ever travelled, it would still take 119,000 years to reach the nearest star.

The Apollo rockets reached 39,500 km/h and at that speed, it would take almost 28,000 years to travel the distance light travels in a year. Alpha Centauri is 4.3 light years away.

264.
Honey is the only food that doesn't spoil.
Source: Smithsonian Magazine.

Honey, though a liquid, contains very little water, is mildly acidic and naturally contains the antiseptic hydrogen peroxide. Ancient Egyptians used honey medicinally on wounds and burns.

265.
The Inuit have 50 words for snow.
Source: washingtonpost.com

Nope, not hundreds as some websites would have you believe but there is about 50.

266.
Hummingbirds are the only birds that can fly backwards.

Source: discovermagazine.com.

And forwards, and hover as well, which is pretty awesome when you think about it.

267.
An ostrich's eye is bigger than its brain.
Source: animals.howstuffworks.com.

Oh and by the way, they don't bury their head in the sand – urban myth!

268.
There is a royal palace in the United States.

Iolani Palace in Honolulu belonged to the kings and queens of Hawaii and served as the only official royal residence in the United States from 1882 to 1893.

269.
It takes less than one second to decide whether you have feelings for someone.
Source: nature.com.

A study done by Syracuse University found it took only 0.2 seconds to release dopamine, oxytocin, adrenaline, and vasopressin, the chemicals in the brain which induce the feeling of love.

270.
Michael Phelps has won more Olympic gold medals than 108 countries.
Michael Phelps won 23 gold medals during his career, scoring more first places than the combined Olympic output of such illustrious countries as Jamaica, Mexico, India and Egypt.

271.
Wilt Chamberlain scored 100 points in an NBA game.
Probably the hardest NBA record to break, Wilt the Stilt scored 100 points in a 167-149 game against the Knicks in 1962. The next closest is Kobe Bryant, who once score 81 points (by the way, Wilt holds the #3, #4 and #5 spots on the list as well with 78, 73 and 72 points in a single game).

272.
Every continent except Africa has hosted the Olympics.
Granted, it would be next to impossible for Africa to host a Winter Olympics, but seriously, the IOC has never awarded a games to any country on this continent?

273.
Water covers 71% of the planet's surface.
And interestingly, we have only explored 5% of the oceans.

274.
Almost two billion people drink contaminated water daily.
Source: World Health Organization.

And it's not just contaminated, it contains feces, which puts them at risk of typhoid, dysentery, cholera and polio.

275.
Three alligators have lived in the White House.
Source: presidentialpetmuseum.com.

Not one, but two presidents have kept alligators as pets. John Quincy Adams was re-gifted one from the Marquis de Lafayette, which he kept in the East Room. Herbert Hoover's son Allan kept two alligators on the White House grounds.

276.
Washington D.C. was built on a mosquito-infested swamp.
Source: Smithsonian Magazine.

FALSE! When the capital was picked out, they chose a dry riverbed, not a festering swamp, which hopefully puts the "Drain the Swamp" euphemism to rest.

277.
"It is unlawful for small boys to throw stones, at any time or place in the District of Columbia."
Source: onlyinyourstate.com.

I suppose larger boys are exempt from this law.

278.
Frank Sinatra almost played John McClane in *Die Hard*.
Sources: yahoo.com, mentalfloss.com

Sinatra played the title role in film adaptation of the book *The Detective* and since *Die Hard* was based on the sequel *Nothing Lasts Forever*, Frank Sinatra had to be offered the role Bruce Willis made famous. At 73 years old, Sinatra wisely turned the role down.

279.
It is a hanging offense in Texas to put graffiti on someone else's cow
Source: mysanantonio.com.

Since a cow is property, defacing it would be considered vandalism and is still punishable by hanging in the Lone Star State.

280.
The lead guitarist from Queen is a rocket scientist.

Ok, he's an astrophysicist, but let's not split hairs. Brian May played with the legendary band for years, but what to do after the death of Freddie Mercury? May had started his PhD in astrophysics before Queen broke out, but put it on the back burner because, well, he was the lead guitarist for Queen. In 2007 he completed his doctorate at Imperial College, London and has consulted on the Deep Horizons project with NASA.

281.

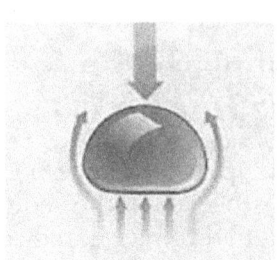

Raindrops are shaped like hamburger buns.
Source: NASA.

As a raindrop fall, friction causes the bottom to flatten which causes it to look more like a hamburger bun, less like a...well a raindrop.

282.

And your grandmother could smell when rain was coming.
Source: livescience.com.

Some plants secrete oils during dry periods, and when it rains, these oils are released into the air.

283.

Sperm counts are less than half what they were in 1971.
Source: independent.co.uk.

Researchers from Israel, Spain, Denmark, Brazil and the U.S. reported in the journal *Human Reproduction Update* total sperm count had fallen 59.3 per cent between 1971 and 2011 in Europe, North America, Australia and New Zealand. Lifestyle and hormone-disrupting chemicals were blamed.

284.

Ernest Hemingway survived anthrax, malaria, pneumonia, dysentery, hepatitis, diabetes, two plane crashes, a ruptured kidney, spleen and liver, a fractured skull and three car crashes, but died by his own hand.

Sources: time.com, *Conversations with Ernest Hemingway, Ernest Hemingway: The Search for Courage, Ernest Hemingway: A Reconsideration,* medicaldaily.com.

Hemingway was wounded in World War I by a mortar shell, taking shrapnel and ending up with an aluminum kneecap. Within the space of two days, he survived two plane crashes in Kenya. He was suffering from anthrax while in Cuba, malaria while working for the *Toronto Star*, dysentery while at Mt. Kilimanjaro, hepatitis (which he was treated for at the Mayo Clinic) and the diabetes from his excessive drinking. The organ ruptures and fractured skull came from the car and plane crashes.

285.
God killed over 2.8 million people in the Bible. Satan killed 10.

Source: dwindlinginunbelief.blogspot.ca.

Take this number as you will, but the owner of this website has itemized all instances in the Bible where God has punished those he sees fit. The number doesn't include those killed during the Great Flood, which the author estimates at 20 million.

286.
The largest office building in the world is in Romania.

The Palace of the Parliament was built during the Ceausescu years as a monument to his megalomania. While the Pentagon has more square feet (6.6 million to the Palace's 3.9 million), it is more of a military installation. The Palace is also the heaviest building in the world, weighing in at around 4.5 million tons (which makes you wonder how it hasn't sunk into the river flowing through Bucharest).

287.
The Sphinx's nose wasn't blown off by Napoleon.
Source: smithsonianjourneys.org

It had been popularly said Napoleon's troops blew off the Sphinx's nose while using it for target practice in the early 1800s. True story is Muhammad Sa'im al-Dahr destroyed it in 1378 when peasants made offerings to the Great Sphinx in the hope of controlling the flood cycle, which angered al-Dahr.

288.
Your ears and nose grow until you die.

Ever wonder why the elderly have larger ears and noses? It's because cartilage – the rubbery substance both are made from – continues to grow until the day you die. Not only does cartilage grow, but the earlobes elongate from gravity. And that makes ears look even larger.

289.
In Japan, you are guilty until proven innocent.
Source: aljazeera.com

So you might want to be careful when travelling there.

290.
The average age of a B-52 bomber is 55 years.
Source: L.A. Times.

The B-52 Stratofortress (or Stratosaurus as some call it) has been around since just after the Korean War and the average age of the fleet of 75 bombers would mean they were built during the *Kennedy Administration!* If that's not weird enough, the U.S. Air Force plans to keep them in service until around 2050, which would mean they will be as old as that oldest lady in the retirement home.

291.
Sean Connery wore a toupee in each of his Bond films.

You may think Sir Sean went bald later in life, but he started losing his hair at 21 and by the time he was cast in *Dr. No*, the bald spot was noticeable, but the producers wanted nobody else – and who else could play 007?

292.
And the guy who played Goldfinger couldn't speak English.
Source: *Goldfinger* documentary.

On the extended DVD version of *Goldfinger*, Honor (Pussy Galore) Blackman tells the story of when Gert Frobe was hired to play the Bond villain. Cubby Broccoli and Harry Saltzman asked him if he could speak English. He nodded, said yes, then when he showed up for the first day of filming, just mouthed the lines (which were dubbed later by English actor Michael Collins).

293.
Andrew Jackson dueled up to 100 times.
Sources: history.com, Washington Post

Ol' Hickory was a feisty president, taking two bullets – one in the chest during a duel in 1806 and the other during a bar fight with a Senator. He killed Charles Dickinson in a duel when he accused Jackson of cheating on a horse race bet and then insulted his wife Rachel.

294.
Martin Van Buren was the first president born in the United States.

The 8th President of the United States was the first born in the new country (the previous seven were born in the British colonies). He was also the first to have English as his second language, learning Dutch as a child.

295.
You swallow eight spiders a year in your sleep.
Source: Scientific American.
FALSE! Unless you have spider food (like flies) in your mouth, never going to happen.

296.
In New Jersey it's illegal to wear a bulletproof vest while committing a crime.
This one sounds incredibly stupid, but there is a reason behind New Jersey statute 2C:39-13 – it adds another crime on to your rap sheet and can push it from a third to second degree crime, raising the jail time.

297.
President James Garfield was ambidextrous and could write in Greek with one hand and in Latin with the other at the same time.
Source: constitutioncenter.org.
Unfortunately, that didn't save him from an assassin's bullet just six months into his presidency.

298.
Alexander Graham Bell invented the metal detector to save Garfield.
Source: metaldetector.com
The legendary inventor came up with his invention and hurried to the White house to locate the bullet. The metal bedsprings kept pinging and the doctors, unimpressed with the invention, just kept cutting and poking around in Garfield's body with their unsterilized hands.

299.
Bell was also the president of National Geographic.
In fact he was the second president, which makes sense since his father-in-law was the founder and first president of the NGS. Bell's descendants have been on the board of the National Geographic Society since and currently his great-great-granddaughter Alexandra serves.

300.
There is more sugar in cranberry juice than in Coke.
Sources: Ocean Spray, Coca-Cola.

A 12 oz. can of Coca-Cola contains 39 grams of sugar, Ocean Spray 100% Cranberry Juice has 42 grams of sugar for the same size serving. To be clear, that's almost a ¼ cup of sugar in your cranberry juice.

301.
The man who invented the Super Soaker also helped develop the Stealth Bomber.
Source: biography.com

In Lonnie Johnson's last year of high school in 1968, he invented a working robot, winning first place at the science fair at the University of Alabama. On an Air Force scholarship he entered Tuskegee U. After university, he worked for NASA on the Galileo mission, the Air Force on the Stealth Bomber, and by accident invented the Super Soaker.

302.
A smartphone is one million times more powerful than the Moon Landing computers.
Sources: Computer Weekly, zmescience.com.

The images of Mission Control are well known – banks of computers guiding the astronauts. Let's put that in perspective. All those machines had a computing capacity of 64KB of memory operating at 0.043MHz. An iPhone has at least 4GB (or 4,000,000KB) and operates at 1.4GHz (or 1,400 MHz). The difference between an iPhone and the NASA computers is the Moon Shot computers were crashproof, and you couldn't play Candy Crush on them.

303.
NASA used to shop on eBay for the Space Shuttle electronics
Source: New York Times.

By the end of their lives, the shuttles' computers were so outdated and since nobody made them anymore, NASA actually had to buy spare parts on websites like eBay.

304.

North Korea makes money by counterfeiting Viagra and $100 U.S. bills.

Source: cbc.ca.

So when you get that email selling cheap Viagra, it's coming from Kim Jong Un himself. The Koreans also traffic cocaine, heroin, fentanyl and crystal meth, because that's what good governments do to cover their budget deficits.

305.
The largest unreinforced concrete dome in the world is 1,900 years old.

The Roman Pantheon was built in 118AD and though Roman concrete is weaker than today's concrete, it sure lasts a hell of a lot longer.

306.
The Queen takes a hostage every time she opens Parliament.

Source: BBC.

Yep, she's a wily old one. Dating back to the 1600s and the English Civil War, the Royals take a Member of Parliament hostage to ensure the safe return of the monarch. It's supposedly quite an honor today.

307.
And the Queen's traditional bodyguard search the basement for gunpowder.
Source: independent.co.uk.

The Searching of the Cellars is the traditional... well...searching of the cellars under Parliament to make sure there isn't a repeat of the 1605 Gunpowder Plot to blow up the House. Ceremonial now, since there's cameras EVERYWHERE.

308.
More people have mobile phones than toilets.
Source: Forbes.

This interesting statistic comes from a U.N. report from 2013. Then (and it's probably worse now) six billion people had mobile phones, but only 4.5 billion had access to a flush toilet.

309.
The U.S. government is still paying a Civil War pension.
Source: U.S. News and World Report.

Sure, the hostilities ended 153 years ago, but as of February 3, 2018, Irene Triplett was still collecting her father's military pension of $73 a month. Mose Triplett served in the Confederate army and fathered Irene when he was 83 and his wife was 33. Wow.

310.
The world's last First World War combat veteran died 93 years after end of the war.

If you think Mose was impressive, let's talk about Claude Choules and Harry Patch, who died in 2011 and 2009, respectively. Claude served in the Australian Navy and Harry survived in the trenches, then lived another 91 years!

311.
Every female Marine who has attempted the qualification course for combat has failed.
Source: uso.org.

Since former Secretary of Defense Leon Panetta ordered the military to integrate women into combat arms occupations in January 2013, more than 18 female infantry officer candidates have. All 18 have failed to qualify.

312.
But 100 men are honorary Marines.
Source: uso.org.

Only the Commandant of the Marine Corps can make someone an honorary Marine. Besides honorary Brigadier General Bob Hope, there is Master Sgt. Bugs Bunny, Corporal Jim Nabors (or as you may know him, Gomer Pyle, U.S.M.C.) and Chuck Norris, who's rank is unknown but, as the USO aptly pointed out, it's also unnecessary – it is, after all, Chuck Norris).

313.
67% of Americans get their news from social media.
Source: journalism.org.

As of 2017, even older people are using social media – 55% of those 50 and older now consult social media to get some of their news.

314.
The U.S. Navy's most advanced ship was commanded by Captain Kirk.

The *USS Zumwalt*, a stealth destroyer was launched in 2013, commanded by Captain James A. Kirk (as opposed to Captain James T. Kirk from *Star Trek*). Captain Kirk was replaced in 2016, though I don't think his replacement was Mr. Spock.

315.
Paul Revere never shouted, "The British are coming!"
Source: history.com.

Sorry Grade 3 history buffs. The most famous line from the American War of Independence was fabricated sometime later. Revere, William Dawes and Samuel Prescott discretely travelled alerting the populace of the British landing.

316.
The United States Army is older than the United States.
Source: mentalfloss.com.

The Second Continental Congress authorized a Continental Army to be led by Major General George Washington. The measure passed on June 14, 1775, over a year before the Declaration of Independence.

317.
China used more cement in three years than the U.S. did in the entire 20th Century.
Source: Washington Post.

Between 1901 and 2000, the United States used 4.5 billion tons of concrete to build bridges, the Interstate system, the Empire State Building, etc. etc. Between 2011 and 2013, China used 6.6 billion tons.

318.
In Alabama it's illegal to drive blindfolded.
Source: foxnews.com.

Which is more stupid: this law, or that they had to write this law because someone was stupid enough to try it.

319.
In Connecticut, a pickle must bounce to be called a pickle.
Source: The Connecticut state library.

FALSE! This urban legend comes from an inspector in 1948 discussing ways to check if a pickle was fit for human consumption, including dropping it one foot and it should bounce. There is no such law.

320.
In Vermont it's illegal for a woman to wear false teeth without her husband's permission.
Source: Reader's Digest

Though looking through the Vermont statutes online, I could find no mention of this law.

321.
Donald Trump is the 45th President, but only the 44th man to be President

What is this witchcraft? Was Andrew Jackson a woman in drag? Was Millard Fillmore really Alec Baldwin travelling from the future? Nope, there's a rather mundane explanation. The walrus-mustached Grover Cleveland was president, voted out, then voted back in again, making him the 22nd and 24th President of the United States (that's what happens when you hold office for two non-consecutive terms)

322.
Grover Cleveland had a rubber jaw.
Source: npr.org.

President 22 and 24 had an upper jaw made of vulcanized rubber, and that's not even the weird part. He ended up with the jaw after a 90-minute secret surgery on a friend's yacht to remove a tumor in his mouth, which had spread to his jaw. The amazing thing is it was kept secret for 24 years.

323.
More than 2 million Americans live on less than $2 a day.
Source: Forbes, Brookings Institute, World Bank.

FALSE! This number comes from the book *$2.00 a Day: Living on Almost Nothing in America* and though some people at some point in the year may live on $2, even the World Bank says it's just not true. The Brookings Institute did their own analysis and found 0.09% of the population does – which is still almost 300,000 people.

324.
94% of paper money is contaminated with bacteria.
Source: National Institute of Health, U.S. Air Force.

Apple Pay, anybody? Some of the bacteria was good, but most was not, including pathogens which cause staph infections, the flu virus, as well as fecal matter, heroin and cocaine.

325.
The top grossing video game of all time is Space Invaders.
Source: businessinsider.com

An oldie but a goodie, Space Invaders – along with Pac Man – probably launched the arcade craze of the 1980s and has grossed $13.9 billion.

326.
McDonald's sells 550 million Big Macs a year in the U.S. alone.
Source: McDonald's.

Sadly, I don't know how many Shrimp Burgers they sell in Korea or Poutine in Canada.

327.
The Big Mac Index is used to measure purchasing power.

Although created as a bit of a joke in 1986 by *The Economist*, it is a fairly accurate way to test your purchasing power in various countries. In case you're wondering, a Big Mac is most expensive in Switzerland at $6.80 and cheapest in the Ukraine at $1.60.

328.
President John Tyler was so hated even his obituary was nasty.

The New York Times called him "the most unpopular public man that had ever held any office in the United States." It could be because he went and joined the Confederacy during the Civil War, which meant even Honest Abe wouldn't acknowledge his predecessor's death in 1862.

329.
You can drink tonic water to combat malaria.

Yes this is true, since tonic water contains quinine, which used to be an anti-malarial drug. But, you would have to drive about five gallons a day to get the prescribed dose of quinine. And since there's no way to drink tonic water without gin or vodka, that's a lot of drinking.

330.
And 7-Up used to contain lithium.
Sources: New York Times, huffingtonpost.com

When it came out in 1929, it was known as "Bib-Label Lithiated Lemon-Lime Soda." The drink had lithium citrate in it, a treatment for bipolar disorder and had the ingredient until 1950 when it had to reformulate due to FDA regulations.

331.
Coca-Cola is responsible for the modern image of Santa Claus.
Sources: snopes.com, publicdomainreview.org.

FALSE! The Santa Claus we see today wasn't influenced by the artist Coke hired in the 1930s. His modern image was already set by the likes of Puck Magazine in 1902 and Norman Rockwell. Coke just built on this.

332.
Anyone who serves on a U.S. Navy submarine is a volunteer.
Source: U.S. Navy.

As a great source of pride, anyone who serves on a submarine – due to its close quarters, claustrophobic atmosphere and lack of privacy, among other things – must volunteer for service.

333.
Bob Barker was a fighter pilot.
Source: navy.togetherweserved.com.

The legendary *The Price is Right* host also served in the U.S. Navy as a fighter pilot during World War II. However, his training ended just as the war did, so he didn't see any actual combat. It is unknown if he drove away in...A NEW CAR!

334.
One billion people visit YouTube every month.
Source: Reuters.

One out of every two people on the internet visit YouTube every month. And, Facebook has 2.2 billion unique users, which would be pretty well everyone on the internet, except that guy I know who took his account down. You know who you are.

335.
You can put your hand in molten lead.
Source: Mythbusters.

Thanks to the Leidenfrost effect, if you dip your hand in water, then molten lead, the thin layer of water on your hand acts as an insulator, but to quote an old reality show: DO NOT TRY THIS AT HOME!

336.
The exhaust of a 747 can flip a school bus.

Source: Mythbusters.

The video on YouTube tells it all. Boeing's own specs on the 747 show when the engines are revved up, they produce winds of 200 miles per hour.

337.
Sharks do not get cancer.

Source: American Museum of Natural History.
FALSE! This one comes from people using shark cartilage as an anti-cancer remedy. It might work, but sharks do get cancer.

338.
The Queen sent her first email in 1976.

Source: wired.com.
Using the codename HME2, Her Majesty Elizabeth II sent the first email on the ARPANET, the military predecessor to the internet.

339.
Agatha Christie originally named one of her books *Ten Little N-words*

I can't even type that word out in good conscience. The book was named that in 1939, then changed to *Ten Little Indians* (because that was much better), then finally in the 1980s to *And Then There Were None*.

340.
Edison failed upwards of 3,000 times while inventing the light bulb.

Source: edison.rutgers.edu/newsletter9.html.
According to an 1890 interview with Harper's, Edison himself said he had tried 3,000 times but only twice was able to get it to work. So keep at it, inventors in waiting!

341.

Superglue was invented by accident.
Another one of those excellent accidents. In 1942, Dr. Harry Coover was trying to make a better gunsight, but found his mix stuck to everything. Not getting the hint, he put it away for six years, then tried again to make an airplane canopy. Finding it a failure again, he was going to abandon it but found it stuck to everything and this time realized there was a use for it. He patented it in 1958 and today we have Krazy Glue.

342.
Most of the Earth is in a state of perpetual darkness.
Source: Mother Earth News.

Because 70% of earth is ocean, and the average depth of the oceans is 12,000 feet, most of the planet is completely dark, since light can't penetrate past 330 feet. But…that's a real stretch, *Mother Earth News*.

343.
The blue-ringed octopus' bite can kill you in minutes.
Source: thecephalopodpage.org.

This octopus is native to southeast Asia and if you're bitten by it, you better have your will made out. The tetrodotoxin in its saliva will start to paralyse you in five to ten minutes, followed by respiratory failure and death.

344.
America's first serial killer was also its worst.

You may have heard of H. H. Holmes, the man who went on a quiet spree during the 1893 World's Fair in Chicago. In his hotel he had false walls and trapdoors which he used to trap people, then torture and kill them. It is estimated he may have killed upwards of 200 people over the course of only a couple of years.

345.
The three main actors in *Rebel Without a Cause* all met an untimely death.
James Dean, 24, died in a car crash, Natalie Wood was 43 when she drowned, and Sal Mineo was 39 when he was stabbed to death while parking his car.

346.
Daniel Boone never wore a coonskin hat.
Source: the Boone Society.
Boone's son Nathan had this to say: "My father, Daniel Boone, always despised the raccoon fur caps and did not wear one himself, as he always had a hat." That hat was a felt one, much like the Quakers wore.

347.
Evel Knievel fractured 433 bones during his daredevil career.
Source: guinnessworldrecords.com
Considering we only have 206 bones, that's one big ouch!

348.
Charles Osborne hiccupped continually for 68 years.
Source: guinnessworldrecords.com, bbc.co.uk.

Poor Charlie started hiccupping in 1922 while weighing a hog and stopped in 1990, clocking about 40 hiccups a minute for the first 20 years or so, then slowing down to a mind-numbing 20. Why? Seems when he lifted the pig he burst a blood vessel in his brain, which damaged the part which inhibits the hiccup response.

349.
A man survived being thrown 1,300 feet by a tornado.
Source: guinnessworldrecords.com.

On March 12, 2006, Matt Suter's mobile home was picked up and thrown across a field while he was in it.

350.
And a woman survived a fall of 33,000 feet.
Sources: BBC, New York Times, Guinness.

The record for luckiest person on the face of the Earth goes to Vesna Vulovic. She survived a midair explosion of a Yugoslav Airlines DC-9 on January 26, 1972 with a fractured skull, two crushed vertebrae, broken pelvis, ribs and both legs. Vesna live another 44 years, dying in 2016.

351.
Mr. Rogers once pleaded with Congress for more money.

The YouTube video of this is awesome. In 1969, the unknown Mr. Rogers (he wore a dark suit and tie for this one – guess the red cardigan was in the wash) went to Washington to ask Congress not to cut the public broadcasting budget. After he spoke for about six minutes, Congress doubled the budget to $20 million.

352.
The United States reached the moon thanks to the Nazis.

One of man's greatest achievements was accomplished in part because of Nazi scientists. The Americans realized as World War II was ending the rocket technology the Nazis had was something they needed, so they spirited 1,600 scientists from the collapsing Third Reich to Fort Bliss, Texas.

353.
The U.S. Cavalry still charged on horses in the 21st century.
Source: militaryhistorynow.com.

In October 2001, the 5th Special Forces Group found the best way to move through the harsh countryside was on horseback. As one Special Forces operator wrote, "I am advising a man on how best to employ light infantry and horse cavalry in the attack against the Taliban T-55 Tanks, armored personnel carriers, artillery, anti-aircraft guns and machine guns… We have done this every day since we hit the ground." And, it was successful.

354.
An American oncologist infected people

with cancer to see how they would react.
Source: Oncology Times, ahrp.org.

Dr. Cornelius Rhoads purposely infected Puerto Ricans with cancer cells, resulting in the death of 13 of them while working for the Rockefeller Institute for Medical Investigations. The institute covered it up, but they couldn't cover up a letter he sent to a colleague: *Porto Ricans are beyond doubt the dirtiest, laziest, most degenerate and thievish race of men ever inhabiting this sphere. What the island needs is not public health work but a tidal wave or something to totally exterminate the population. I have done my best to further the process of extermination by killing off eight and transplanting cancer into several more.* Rhoads later left Puerto Rico to head the U.S. Army Biological Weapons division

355.
Nixon persuaded the South Vietnamese to not entertain a peace plan until after he was elected.
Source: New York Times.

Seems there was no end to Tricky Dick's chicanery. During Richard Nixon's campaign for president in 1968, he secretly requested the South Vietnamese leaders not make peace with the United States until after the election, thereby hobbling Vice President Hubert Humphrey's chances.

356.
Saddam Hussein was the biggest bank robber in history.
Sources: New York Daily News, The Independent.

Betcha didn't know that about the Iraqi dictator. The funny thing is, Saddam robbed his own bank when he ordered his son to clean $1 billion in American $100 bills out of the Iraqi Central Bank., which he did by handing a handwritten note from his daddy to the bank's security staff. About a third ($350 million) is still missing.

357.
Hockey is legally Canada's national sport.
The National Sports of Canada Act clearly states: "The game commonly known as ice hockey is hereby recognized and declared to be the national winter sport of Canada."

358.
Obi Wan Kenobi hated *Star Wars*.
Sir Alec Guinness is quoted in his biography as saying it was "fairy-tale rubbish" and "new rubbish dialogue reaches me every other day and none of it makes my character clear or even bearable." But he did think that Tennyson Ford guy was probably amusing. Tennyson Ford?

359.
But he was smart, negotiating 2% of the movie's profits.
Sir Alec's estate (he died in 2000) still turns quite a profit and has made about $50 million over the years. James Earl Jones was paid $5,000 for the iconic Darth Vader voice – and that's it.

360.
If you think he was smart, how about George Lucas.
Source: celebritynetworth.com.

George was entitled to half a million as the director of Star Wars. Instead, he took $150,000 and 100% of all Star Wars merchandise and any future sequels. Of course, 20th Century Fox thought it couldn't lose on that one...except the franchise has made $27 billion worldwide from sequels, licensing and merchandise and George is now worth about $5.2 billion.

361.
Two people have won both a Nobel prize and an Oscar.

Legendary playwright George Bernard Shaw won the 1925 Nobel for literature and the 1938 Oscar for Best Writing. Bob Dylan won an Oscar in 2000 for Best Song and the 2016 Nobel for Literature. Now, if you've won a Grammy, you have a much better chance at a Nobel prize (or is it the other way around), since five people have won both (Mikhail Gorbachev, Jimmy Carter, Barack Obama, Dr. Martin Luther King and yep, you guessed it, Bob Dylan).

362.
A college football coach is the highest paid public employee in 26 states.
Source: espn.com.

In 13 of the other 50 states, it's a basketball coach. The highest is Jim Harbaugh, coach of the Michigan State Wolverines, who pulls in $9 million a year. By contrast, the highest non-coach on the list is a neurosurgeon from Hawaii who makes a paltry $786,000.

363.
In the Grand Canyon, the U.S. Postal Service still delivers mail by mule
Source: Smithsonian Insider.

Because, how else are you supposed to get mail to the bottom of the canyon?

364.
The FBI used falafel purchases to find Iranian secret agents.

Source: wired.com.

In 2005 and '06, the FBI pored over grocery purchases in San Francisco and San Jose, looking for a spike in falafel sales, assuming that would lead to Iranian secret agents in the area. It is unclear if they would check for British terrorists by looking for steak and kidney pie sales as well.

365.
The FBI considered *It's a Wonderful Life* to be communist propaganda

Source: The Atlantic.

From its release in 1946 until 1956, the Christmas classic was on the FBI list of "suspected Communist propaganda," due to its "subversive anti-capitalist/banking themes."

www.ingramcontent.com/pod-product-compliance
Lightning Source LLC
Chambersburg PA
CBHW070434010526
44118CB00014B/2037